Let Evening Come

Other Books by Jane Kenyon

THE BOAT OF QUIET HOURS

FROM ROOM TO ROOM

TWENTY POEMS OF ANNA AKHMATOVA

Let Evening Come

POEMS BY JANE KENYON

GRAYWOLF PRESS · SAINT PAUL · 1990

The poems in this book first appeared in the following magazines: *American Voice, The Atlantic, Harvard Magazine, Iowa Review, Kenyon Review, Missouri Review, The Nation, New Criterion, New Letters, Ohio Review, Ploughshares, Seneca, Virginia Quarterly Review.*

"Heavy Summer Rain," "At the Public Market Museum: Charleston, South Carolina," "The Letter," "Now Where?" and "Private Beach" first appeared in the *New Yorker.*

"After an Illness, Walking the Dog," "The Blue Bowl," "On the Aisle," and "Three Songs at the End of Summer" first appeared in *Poetry.*

The author wishes to give special thanks to Joyce Peseroff and Alice Mattison, Robert Richman, and, as ever, to Donald Hall.

Publication of this volume is made possible in part by grants from the National Endowment for the Arts and the Minnesota State Arts Board. Graywolf Press is the recipient of a McKnight Foundation Award administered by the Minnesota State Arts Board and receives generous contributions from corporations, foundations, and individuals. Graywolf Press is a member agency of United Arts, Saint Paul.

Published by
Graywolf Press
2402 University Avenue, Suite 203
Saint Paul, Minnesota 55114. All rights reserved.

Library of Congress Cataloging-in-Publication Data
Kenyon, Jane.
Let evening come : poems / by Jane Kenyon.
    p. cm.
ISBN I-55597-130-X : $16.95. − ISBN I-55597-131-8 (PBK.) : $11.00
I. Title.
811'.54–dc 20   89-77979

9 8 7 6 5 4

For Pauline Kenyon

Contents

Let Evening Come

"So strange, life is. Why people do not go around
in a continual state of surprise is beyond me."

— WILLIAM MAXWELL

Three Songs at the End of Summer

A second crop of hay lies cut
and turned. Five gleaming crows
search and peck between the rows.
They make a low, companionable squawk,
and like midwives and undertakers
possess a weird authority.

Crickets leap from the stubble,
parting before me like the Red Sea.
The garden sprawls and spoils.

Across the lake the campers have learned
to water ski. They have, or they haven't.
Sounds of the instructor's megaphone
suffuse the hazy air. "Relax! Relax!"

Cloud shadows rush over drying hay,
fences, dusty lane, and railroad ravine.
The first yellowing fronds of goldenrod
brighten the margins of the woods.

Schoolbooks, carpools, pleated skirts;
water, silver-still, and a vee of geese.

*

The cicada's dry monotony breaks
over me. The days are bright
and free, bright and free.

Then why did I cry today
for an hour, with my whole
body, the way babies cry?

*

A white, indifferent morning sky,
and a crow, hectoring from its nest
high in the hemlock, a nest as big
as a laundry basket...
                              In my childhood
I stood under a dripping oak,
while autumnal fog eddied around my feet,
waiting for the school bus
with a dread that took my breath away.

The damp dirt road gave off
this same complex organic scent.

I had the new books – words, numbers,
and operations with numbers I did not
comprehend – and crayons, unspoiled
by use, in a blue canvas satchel
with red leather straps.

Spruce, inadequate, and alien
I stood at the side of the road.
It was the only life I had.

After the Hurricane

I walk the fibrous woodland path to the pond.
Acorns break from the oaks, drop
through amber autumn air
which does not stir. The dog runs way ahead.

I find him snuffling on the shore
among water weeds that detached in the surge;
a broad, soft band of rufous pine needles;
a bar of sand; and shards of mica
glinting in the bright but tepid sun.

Here, really, we had only hard rain.
The cell I bought for the lamp
and kettles of water I drew remain
unused. All day we were restless, drowsy,
afraid, and finally, let down:
we didn't get to demonstrate our grit.

In the full, still pond the likeness
of golden birch leaves and the light they emit
shines exact. When the dog sees himself
his hackles rise. I stir away his trouble
with a stick.

A crow breaks in upon our satisfaction.
We look up to see it lift heavily
from its nest high in the hemlock, and the bough
equivocate in the peculiar light. It was
the author of *Walden*, wasn't it,
who made a sacrament of saying no.

After Working Long on One Thing

Through the screen door
I hear a hummingbird, inquiring
for nectar among the stalwart

hollyhocks – an erratic flying
ruby, asking for sweets among
the sticky-throated flowers.

The sky won't darken in the west
until ten. Where shall I turn
this light and tired mind?

Waking in January Before Dawn

Something that sounded like the town
plow just went by: there must be snow.

What was it I fell asleep thinking
while the shutters strained on their hooks
in the wind, and the window frames
creaked as they do when it's terribly cold,
and getting colder fast? I pulled
the covers over my head.

Now through lace curtains I can see
the huge Wolf Moon going down,
and soon the sky will lighten, turning
first gray, then pink, then blue. . . .

How frightened I was as a child, waking
at Grandma's, though I saw
that the animal about to pounce
—a dreadful, vaguely organized beast—
was really the sewing machine.

Now the dresser reclaims visibility,
and yesterday's clothes cohere
humpbacked and headless on the chair.

Catching Frogs

I crouched beside the deepest pool,
and the smell of damp and moss
rose rich between my knees. Water-striders
creased the silver-black silky surface.
Rapt, I hardly breathed. Gnats
roiled in a shaft of sun.

Back again after supper I'd see
a nose poke up by the big flat stone
at the lip of the fall; then the humped
eyes and the slippery emerald head,
freckled brown. The buff membrane
pulsed under the jaw while
subtleties of timing played in my mind.

With a patience that came like grace
I waited. Mosquitoes moaned all
around. Better to wait. Better to reach
from behind... It grew dark.

I came into the warm, bright room
where father held aloft the evening
paper, and there was talk, and maybe
laughter, though I don't remember laughter.

In the Grove: The Poet at Ten

She lay on her back in the timothy
and gazed past the doddering
auburn heads of sumac.

A cloud – huge, calm,
and dignified – covered the sun
but did not, could not, put it out.

The light surged back again.

Nothing could rouse her then
from that joy so violent
it was hard to distinguish from pain.

The Pear

There is a moment in middle age
when you grow bored, angered
by your middling mind,
afraid.

That day the sun
burns hot and bright,
making you more desolate.

It happens subtly, as when a pear
spoils from the inside out,
and you may not be aware
until things have gone too far.

Christmas Away from Home

Her sickness brought me to Connecticut.
Mornings I walk the dog: that part of life
is intact. Who's painted, who's insulated
or put siding on, who's burned the lawn
with lime – that's the news on Ardmore Street.

The leaves of the neighbor's respectable
rhododendrons curl under in the cold.
He has backed the car
through the white nimbus of its exhaust
and disappeared for the day.

In the hiatus between mayors
the city has left leaves in the gutters,
and passing cars lift them in maelstroms.

We pass the house two doors down, the one
with the wildest lights in the neighborhood,
an establishment without irony.
All summer their *putto* empties a water jar,
their St. Francis feeds the birds.
Now it's angels, festoons, waist-high
candles, and swans pulling sleighs.

Two hundred miles north I'd let the dog
run among birches and the black shade of pines.
I miss the hills, the woods and stony
streams, where the swish of jacket sleeves

against my sides seems loud, and a crow
caws sleepily at dawn.

By now the streams must run under a skin
of ice, white air-bubbles passing erratically,
like blood cells through a vein. Soon the mail,
forwarded, will begin to reach me here.

Taking Down the Tree

"Give me some light!" cries Hamlet's
uncle mid-way through the murder
of Gonzago. "Light! Light!" cry scattering
courtesans. Here, as in Denmark,
it's dark at four, and even the moon
shines with only half a heart.

The ornaments go down into the box:
the silver spaniel, *My Darling*
on its collar, from mother's childhood
in Illinois; the balsa jumping jack
my brother and I fought over,
pulling limb from limb. Mother
drew it together again with thread
while I watched, feeling depraved
at the age of ten.

With something more than caution
I handle them, and the lights, with their
tin star-shaped reflectors, brought along
from house to house, their pasteboard
toy suitcase increasingly flimsy.
Tick, tick, the desiccated needles drop.

By suppertime all that remains is the scent
of balsam fir. If it's darkness
we're having, let it be extravagant.

Dark Morning: Snow

It falls on the vole, nosing somewhere
through weeds, and on the open
eye of the pond. It makes the mail
come late.

The nuthatch spirals head first
down the tree.

I'm sleepy and benign in the dark.
There's nothing I want. . . .

Small Early Valentine

Wind plays the spy,
opens and closes doors,
looks behind shutters –
a succession of clatters. I
know perfectly well
where you are: in that
not-here-place you go to,
the antipodes. I have your note
with flights and phone numbers
for the different days. . . .
Dear one, I have made the bed
with the red sheets. Our
dog's the one who lay
on the deep pile of dung,
lifting his head and ears
when after twenty years
Odysseus approached him.

After the Dinner Party

A late-blooming burgundy hollyhock sways
across the kitchen window in a light breeze
as I draw a tumbler of well-water at the sink.
We're face to face, as in St. Paul's Epistles
or the later novels of Henry James.

The cold rains of autumn have begun.
Driving to Hanover I must have seen
a thousand frogs in the headlights
crossing the gleaming road. Like sheep urged
by a crouching dog they converged
and flowed, as they do every fall.
I couldn't help hitting some.

At dinner I laughed with the rest,
but in truth I prefer the sound
of pages turning, and coals shifting
abruptly in the stove. I left before ten
pleading a long drive home.

The smell of woodsmoke hung
over the small villages along the way.

I passed the huge cold gray stone
buildings left by the chaste Shakers.
Any window will still open with one finger.
Hands to work, and hearts to God . . .

Why do people give dinner parties? Why did I
say I'd come? I suppose no one there was entirely
at ease. Again the flower leans this way:
you know it's impolite to stare. I'll put
out the light. . . . And there's an end to it.

Leaving Barbados

Just as the sun pitched summarily over
the edge of the world we arrived a week
ago. In the afterglow the sunburnt guests
finished their drinks by the pool.

That night we ate breadfruit, yams,
and flying fish in a dining room
with potted palms for walls. Beyond
the shoals a schooner, its rigging strung
with lights, passed by under moon and stars.
A scrawny kitten mewed beneath our chairs.

Letting go into sleep ... the sound of crockery
being stacked in the kitchen, surf and wind.
A small dog barked inconclusively.

Next morning walking on the beach
I caught a whiff of marijuana mingled
with the reek of chicken coops, then
something like sterno, and fire.
Morning glories ramped over a tumbledown house.

Back at the hotel we settled in.
Levon came every day, wearing his tee shirt
that looked like the front of a tux –
which I saw one day drying on a porch
down the beach – and his heart-shaped
sunglasses, pushed back on his leonine
head so I could see his eyes, which were kind.
Cigarettes – funny cigarettes – he'd be your man.

Afternoons he surfed,
his beat-up board secured to his ankle

by a long strap. Perhaps that's how
the long scar came to be on his thigh.
The wind was up; the surf was loud and high.

Now our taxi strains uphill, its doors
ajog, then rushes down the narrow lane.
In the cut-over cane two egrets strut and peck.

Goodbye Barbados – goodbye water, hiss
and thunder; scented winds; clattering palms;
stupefying sun and rum; goodbye turquoise,
pink, copen, lavender, black and red.
Tonight another couple will sleep in our bed.

The Blue Bowl

Like primitives we buried the cat
with his bowl. Bare-handed
we scraped sand and gravel
back into the hole.
                    They fell with a hiss
and thud on his side,
on his long red fur, the white feathers
between his toes, and his
long, not to say aquiline, nose.

We stood and brushed each other off.
There are sorrows keener than these.

Silent the rest of the day, we worked,
ate, stared, and slept. It stormed
all night; now it clears, and a robin
burbles from a dripping bush
like the neighbor who means well
but always says the wrong thing.

The Letter

Bad news arrives in her distinctive hand.
The cancer has returned, this time
to his brain. Surgery impossible,
treatments underway. Hair loss, bouts
of sleeplessness and agitation at night,
exhaustion during the day . . .

I snap the blue leash onto the D-ring
of the dog's collar, and we cross
Route 4, then cut through the hayfield
to the pond road, where I let him run
along with my morbidity.

The trees have leafed out – only just –
and the air is misty with sap.
So green, so brightly, richly succulent,
this arbor over the road . . .
Sunlight penetrates in golden drops.

We come to the place where a neighbor
is taking timber from his land.
There's a smell of lacerated earth
and pine. Hardwood smells different.
His truck is gone.

Now you can see well up the slope,
see ledges of rock and ferns breaking forth
among the stumps and cast-aside limbs
and branches.

The place will heal itself in time, first
with weeds – goldenrod, cinquefoil, moth
mullein, then blackberries, sapling

pine, deciduous trees ... but for now
the dog rolls, jovial, in the pungent
disturbance of wood and earth.

I summon him with a word, turn back,
and we go the long way home.

We Let the Boat Drift

I set out for the pond, crossing the ravine
where seedling pines start up like sparks
between the disused rails of the Boston and Maine.

The grass in the field would make a second crop
if early autumn rains hadn't washed
the goodness out. After the night's hard frost
it makes a brittle rustling as I walk.

The water is utterly still. Here and there
a black twig sticks up. It's five years today,
and even now I can't accept what cancer did
to him – not death so much as the annihilation
of the whole man, sense by sense, thought
by thought, hope by hope.

Once we talked about the life to come.
I took the Bible from the nightstand
and offered John 14: "I go to prepare
a place for you." "Fine. Good," he said.
"But what about Matthew? 'You, therefore,
must be perfect, as your heavenly Father
is perfect.'" And he wept.

My neighbor honks and waves driving by.
She counsels troubled students; keeps bees;
her goats follow her to the mailbox.

Last Sunday afternoon we went canoeing on the pond.
Something terrible at school had shaken her.
We talked quietly far from shore. The paddles

rested across our laps; glittering drops
fell randomly from their tips. The light
around us seemed alive. A loon – itinerant –
let us get quite close before it dove, coming up
after a long time, and well away from humankind.

Spring Changes

The autumnal drone of my neighbor
cutting wood across the pond
and the soundlessness of winter
give way to hammering. Must be
he's roofing, or building a shed
or fence. Some form of spring-induced
material advance.

Mother called early to say she's sold the house.
I'll fly out, help her sort and pack,
and give and throw away. One thing I'd like:
the yellow hand-painted pottery
vase that's crimped at the edge
like the crust of a pie — so gay, but
they almost never used it, who knows why?

A new young pair will paint and mow,
and fix the picket fence, wash windows face
to face in May, he outside on a ladder,
she inside on a chair, mouthing kisses
and "Be Careful!" through the glass.

Insomnia

The almost disturbing scent
of peonies presses through the screens,
and I know without looking how
those heavy white heads lean down
under the moon's light. A cricket chafes
and pauses, chafes and pauses,
as if distracted or preoccupied.

When I open my eyes to document
my sleeplessness by the clock, a point
of greenish light pulses near the ceiling.
A firefly . . . In childhood I ran out
at dusk, a jar in one hand, lid
pierced with airholes in the other,
getting soaked to the knees
in the long wet grass.

The light moves unsteadily, like someone
whose balance is uncertain after traveling
many hours, coming a long way.
Get up. Get up and let it out.

But I leave it hovering overhead, in case
it's my father, come back from the dead
to ask, "Why are you still awake? You can
put grass in their jar in the morning."

April Chores

When I take the chilly tools
from the shed's darkness, I come
out to a world made new
by heat and light.

The snake basks and dozes
on a large flat stone.
It reared and scolded me
for raking too close to its hole.

Like a mad red brain
the involute rhubarb leaf
thinks its way up
through loam.

The Clearing

The dog and I push through the ring
of dripping junipers
to enter the open space high on the hill
where I let him off the leash.

He vaults, snuffling, between tufts of moss;
twigs snap beneath his weight; he rolls
and rubs his jowls on the aromatic earth;
his pink tongue lolls.

I look for sticks of proper heft
to throw for him, while he sits, prim
and earnest in his love, if it is love.

All night a soaking rain, and now the hill
exhales relief, and the fragrance
of warm earth. . . . The sedges
have grown an inch since yesterday,
and ferns unfurled, and even if they try
the lilacs by the barn can't
keep from opening today.

I longed for spring's thousand tender greens,
and the white-throated sparrow's call
that borders on rudeness. Do you know —
since you went away
all I can do
is wait for you to come back to me.

Work

It has been light since four. In June
the birds find plenty to remark upon
at that hour. Pickup trucks, three men
to a cab, rush past burgeoning hay
and corn to summer constructions
up in town.
                    Here, soon, the mowing, raking
and baling will begin. And I must tell
how, before the funeral all those years ago,
we lay down briefly on your grandparents'
bed, and that when you stood to put on
your jacket the change slipped
from your pants pocket.

Some dropped on the chenille
spread, and some hit the thread-bare rug,
and one coin rolled onto the wide pine
floorboard under the dresser, hit
the molding, teetered and fell silent
like the rest. And oh, your sigh —
the sigh you sighed then...

Private Beach

It is always the dispossessed –
someone driving a huge rusted Dodge
that's burning oil, and must cost
twenty-five dollars to fill.

Today before seven I saw, through
the morning fog, his car leave the road,
turning into the field. It must be
his day off, I thought, or he's out
of work and drinking, or getting stoned.
Or maybe as much as anything
he wanted to see
where the lane through the hay goes.

It goes to the bluff overlooking
the lake, where we've cleared
brush, swept the slippery oak
leaves from the path, and tried to destroy
the poison ivy that runs
over the scrubby, sandy knolls.

Sometimes in the evening I'll hear
gunshots or firecrackers. Later a car
needing a new muffler backs out
to the road, headlights withdrawing
from the lowest branches of the pines.

Next day I find beer cans, crushed;
sometimes a few fish too small
to bother cleaning and left
on the moss to die; or the leaking
latex trace of outdoor love. . . .

Once I found the canvas sling chairs
broken up and burned.

Whoever laid the fire gathered stones
to contain it, like a boy pursuing
a merit badge, who has a dream of work,
and proper reward for work.

At the Spanish Steps in Rome

Keats had come with his friend Severn
for the mild Roman winter. Afternoons
they walked to the Borghese Gardens
to see fine ladies, nannies with babies,
and handsome mounted officers,
whose horses moved sedately
along the broad and sandy paths.

But soon the illness kept him in.
Severn kept trying in that stoutly
cheerful English way: he rented a spinet,
hauled it three flights, turning it end
up on the landings, and played Haydn every day.

Love letters lay unopened in a chest.
"To see her hand writing would break my heart."

The poet's anger rose as his health sank.
He began to refer to his "posthumous
existence." One day while Severn and the porter
watched he flung, dish by dish, his catered
meal into the street.

Now the room where Keats died is a museum,
closed for several hours midday with the rest
of Rome. Waiting on the Steps in the wan
October sun I see the curator's pale,
exceptionally round face looking down.
Everything that was not burned that day
in accordance with the law is there.

Waiting

At the grocery store on a rainy July day
I pull in beside a family wagon:
Connecticut plates but no luggage —
summer people then, up for bright days
and cool nights, and local church fairs.
They may have been coming here for years.

Three little boys and a golden retriever
are steaming up the windows already smudged
by the dog's nose. The smallest boy
pitches himself repeatedly over the seat,
arms and legs flying, like some rubbery toy.
From time to time the dog woofs abstractedly.

Inside I look for their mother. And what
about their father — is he here too, or does he
come only on weekends and holidays
from Stamford, Farmington, or Darien?

There she is: of the right age, dressed
expensively, stiffly, carrying a straw
summer bag with a scrimshaw whale on the lid,
a hard little basket out of which she draws
a single large bill for the food. Clearly
this time she's come alone.

She will fill the cottage cupboards
and refrigerator, settle the boys
on the sleeping porch with one bunk bed

and one cot, and arbitrate the annual fight
over who gets to sleep on top.

And she will wait. Life is odd. . . .
I too am waiting, though if you asked
what for, I wouldn't know what to say.

Staying at Grandma's

Sometimes they left me for the day
while they went – what does it matter
where – away. I sat and watched her work
the dough, then turn the white shape
yellow in a buttered bowl.

A coleus, wrong to my eye because its leaves
were red, was rooting on the sill
in a glass filled with water and azure
marbles. I loved to see the sun
pass through the blue.

"You know," she'd say, turning
her straight and handsome back to me,
"that the body is the temple
of the Holy Ghost."

The Holy Ghost, the oh, oh ... the *uh
oh,* I thought, studying the toe of my new shoe,
and glad she wasn't looking at me.

Soon I'd be back in school. No more mornings
at Grandma's side while she swept the walk
or shook the dust mop by the neck.

If she loved me why did she say that
two women would be grinding at the mill,
that God would come out of the clouds
when they were least expecting him,
choose one to be with him in heaven
and leave the other there alone?

Church Fair

Who knows what I might find
on tables under the maple trees —
perhaps a saucer in Aunt Lois's china pattern
to replace the one I broke
the summer I was thirteen, and visiting
for a week. Never in all these years
have I thought of it without
a warm surge of embarrassment.

I'll go through the closets and cupboards
to find things for the auction.
I'll bake a peach pie for the food table,
and rolls for the supper,
Grandma Kenyon's recipe, which came down to me
along with her legs and her brooding disposition.
"Mrs. Kenyon," the doctor used to tell her,
"you are simply killing yourself with work."
This she repeated often, with keen satisfaction.

She lived to be a hundred and three,
surviving all her children,
including the one so sickly at birth
that she had to carry him everywhere on a pillow
for the first four months. Father
suffered from a weak chest — bronchitis,
pneumonias, and pleurisy — and early on
books and music became his joy.

Surely these clothes are from another life —
not my own. I'll drop them off on the way
to town. I'm getting the peaches
today, so they'll be ripe by Saturday.

A Boy Goes into the World

My brother rode off on his bike
into the summer afternoon, but
mother called me back
from the end of the sandy drive:
"It's different for girls."

He'd be gone for hours, come back
with things: a cocoon, gray-brown
and papery around a stick;
a puff ball, ripe, wrinkled,
and exuding spores; owl pellets –
bits of undigested bone and fur;
and pieces of moss that might
have made toupees for preposterous
green men, but went instead
into a wide-necked jar for a terrarium.

He mounted his plunder on poster
board, gluing and naming
each piece. He has long since
forgotten those days and things, but
I at last can claim them as my own.

The Three Susans

Ancient maples mingle over us, leaves
the color of pomegranates.
The days are warm with honey light,
but the last two nights have finished
every garden in the village.

The provident have left green tomatoes
to ripen on newspaper in the darkness of sheds.
The peppers were already in.
Now there will be no more corn.

I let myself through the wrought iron gate
of the graveyard, and – meaning to exclude
the dog – I close it after me. But he runs
to the other end, and jumps the stone
wall overlooking Elbow Pond.

Here Samuel Smith lay down at last
with his three wives, all named Susan.
I had to see it for myself. They died
in their sixties, one outliving him.
So why do I feel indignant? He suffered.
Love and the Smiths' peculiar fame
"to nothingness do sink." And down the row
Sleepers are living up to their name.

The dog cocks his leg on a stone.
But animals do not mock, and the dead
may be glad to have life breaking in.

The sun drops low over the pond.
Long shadows move out from the stones,

and a chill rises from the moss,
prompt as a deacon. And at Keats's grave
in the Protestant cemetery in Rome
it is already night,
and wild cats are stalking in the moat.

Learning in the First Grade

"The cup is red. The drop of rain
is blue. The clam is brown."

So said the sheet of exercises –
purple mimeos, still heady
from the fluid in the rolling
silver drum. But the cup was

not red. It was white,
or had no color of its own.

Oh, but my mind was finical.
It put the teacher perpetually
in the wrong. Called on, however,
I said aloud: "The cup is red."

"But it's not," I thought,
like Galileo Galilei
muttering under his beard. . . .

At the Public Market Museum:
Charleston, South Carolina

A volunteer, a Daughter of the Confederacy,
receives my admission and points the way.
Here are gray jackets with holes in them,
red sashes with individual flourishes,
things soft as flesh. Someone sewed
the gold silk cord onto that gray sleeve
as if embellishments
could keep a man alive.

I have been reading *War and Peace*,
and so the particulars of combat
are on my mind – the shouts and groans
of men and boys, and the horses' cries
as they fall, astonished at what
has happened to them.
                              Blood on leaves,
blood on grass, on snow; extravagant
beauty of red. Smoke, dust of disturbed
earth; parch and burn.

Who would choose this for himself?
And yet the terrible machinery
waited in place. With psalters
in their breast pockets, and gloves
knitted by their sisters and sweethearts,
the men in gray hurled themselves
out of the trenches, and rushed against
blue. It was what both sides
agreed to do.

Lines for Akhmatova

The night train from Moscow, beginning to slow,
pulled closer to your sleeping city.
A sound like tiny bells in cold air... Then
the attendant appeared with glasses of strong tea.
"Wake up, ladies! This is Leningrad."

The narrow canals gleam black and still
under ornate street lamps, and in the parks
golden leaves lie on the sandy paths
and wooden benches. By light of day
old women dressed in black sweep them away
with birch stick brooms.

Your work, your amorous life, your scholarship –
everything happened here, where the Party
silenced you for twenty-five years
for writing about love – a middle-class activity.

Husband and son, lovers, dear companions
were imprisoned or killed, emigrated or died.
You turned still further inward,
imperturbable as a lion-gate, and lived on
stubbornly, learning Dante by heart.

In the end you outlived the genocidal
Georgian with his moustache thick as a snake.
And in triumph, an old woman, you wrote:
I can't tell if the day is ending, or the world,
or if the secret of secrets is within me again.

Heavy Summer Rain

The grasses in the field have toppled,
and in places it seems that a large, now
absent, animal must have passed the night.
The hay will right itself if the day

turns dry. I miss you steadily, painfully.
None of your blustering entrances
or exits, doors swinging wildly
on their hinges, or your huge unconscious
sighs when you read something sad,
like Henry Adams's letters from Japan,
where he travelled after Clover died.

Everything blooming bows down in the rain:
white irises, red peonies; and the poppies
with their black and secret centers
lie shattered on the lawn.

September Garden Party

We sit with friends at the round
glass table. The talk is clever;
everyone rises to it. Bees
come to the spiral pear peelings
on your plate.
From my lap or your hand
the spice of our morning's privacy
comes drifting up. Fall sun
passes through the wine.

While We Were Arguing

The first snow fell – or should I say
it flew slantwise, so it seemed
to be the house
that moved so heedlessly through space.

Tears splashed and beaded on your sweater.
Then for long moments you did not speak.
No pleasure in the cups of tea I made
distractedly at four.

The sky grew dark. I heard the paper come
and went out. The moon looked down
between disintegrating clouds. I said
aloud: "You see, we have done harm."

Dry Winter

So little snow that the grass in the field
like a terrible thought
has never entirely disappeared ...

On the Aisle

Leaving Maui – orchids on our plates,
whales seen from the balcony at cocktail hour,
and Mai Tais bristling with fruit –
we climb through thirty-two thousand feet
with retired schoolteachers, widows on tours,
and honeymooners. The man and woman next to me,
young, large, bronze, and prosperous,
look long without fear or shame
into each other's faces.

Anxious, I am grateful for rum, my last
island draught, and the circulation
of the blood, and I begin Gogol's story
about a painter whose love of luxury
destroys his art. People pull down
their window shades, shutting out the sun,
and a movie called *Clue* comes on.
I continue to read in my pillar of light
like a village schoolmistress, while
from the dark on my right comes
the sound of kissing. It would be a lie
to say I didn't sneak a look.

On the slow approach to rainy San Francisco
I find I had things figured wrong:
"Don't worry, ok? He's still out of town."
I stop speculating about their occupations
and combined income. They fall silent again.

We hit the runway and bounce three times.
After what seems too long the nose comes down;
I feel the brakes go on. Their grief is real
when my seatmates part at the gate. He has
a close connection to Tucson,
and runs for it.

At the Winter Solstice

The pines look black in the half-
light of dawn. Stillness ...
While we slept an inch of new snow
simplified the field. Today of all days
the sun will shine no more
than is strictly necessary.

At the village church last night
the boys – shepherds and wisemen –
pressed close to the manger in obedience,
wishing only for time to pass;
but the girl dressed as Mary trembled
as she leaned over the pungent hay,
and like the mother of Christ
wondered why she had been chosen.

After the pageant, a ruckus of cards,
presents, and homemade Christmas sweets.
A few of us stayed to clear the bright
scraps and ribbons from the pews,
and lift the pulpit back in place.

When I opened the hundred-year-old Bible
to Luke's account of the Epiphany
black dust from the binding rubbed off
on my hands, and on the altar cloth.

The Guest

I had opened the draft on the stove
and my head was tending downward when
a portly housefly dropped on the page
in front of me. Confused by the woodstove's
heat, the fly, waking ill-tempered, lay
on its back, flailing its legs and wings.

Then it lurched into the paper clips.
The morning passed, and I forgot about
my guest, except when the buzz rose
and quieted, rose and quieted – tires
spinning on ice, chainsaw far away,
someone carrying on alone. . . .

Father and Son

August. My neighbor started cutting wood
on cool Sabbath afternoons, the blue
plume of the saw's exhaust wavering over
his head. At first I didn't mind the noise
but it came to seem like a species of pain.

From time to time he let the saw idle,
stepping back from the logs and aromatic
dust, while his son kicked the billets
down the sloping drive toward the shed.
In the lull they sometimes talked.

His back ached unrelentingly, he assumed
from all the stooping. Sundays that fall
they bent over the pile of beech and maple,
intent on getting wood for winter, the last,
as it happened, of their life together.

Three Crows

Three crows fly across a gun–metal
sky. Turgenev, in love for forty years
with Pauline Viardot . . .

Paris, Baden, wherever she and Louis lived
the writer followed, writing books
in which love invariably goes awry.
The men hunted small game companionably.

Spring rain, relentless as obsession:
the mountain streams run swift and full.
The red tassles of blossoming maples
hang bright against wet black bark.

"I lived," he said, "all my life
on the edge of another's nest."

Spring Snow

A thoughtful snow comes falling ...
seems to hang in the air before
concluding that it must fall
here. Huge aggregate flakes

alight on the muddy ruts
of March, and the standing
water that thaws by day
and freezes by night.

Venus is content to shine unseen
this evening, having risen serene
above springs, and false springs.
But I, restless after supper, pace

the long porch while the snow falls,
dodging the clothesline I won't
use until peonies send up red,
plump, irrepressible spears.

Ice Out

As late as yesterday ice preoccupied
the pond – dark, half-melted, water-logged.
Then it sank in the night, one piece,
taking winter with it. And afterward
everything seems simple and good.

All afternoon I lifted oak leaves
from the flowerbeds, and greeted
like friends the green-white crowns
of perennials. They have the tender,
unnerving beauty of a baby's head.

How I hated to come in! I've left
the windows open to hear the peepers'
wildly disproportionate cries.
Dinner is over, no one stirs. The dog
sighs, sneezes, and closes his eyes.

Going Away

Like Varya in *The Cherry Orchard*
I keep the keys, and go around locking
the new deadbolts, meant to ward off
antique thieves: loud, satisfying clicks.

When I am walking down some broad, linden-
lined boulevard where people pass
whole afternoons at tables in dappled
shade, and where the cries of news vendors

mean nothing to me, I'll be glad
that I've overwatered all the plants,
stopped the mail, and wound the clock
to tick and chime as if I were at home.

The dog has understood the melancholy
meaning of open satchels and has hurled
himself down by the door, hoping not to be
left in the silent house, like Firs. . . .

Now Where?

It wakes when I wake, walks
when I walk, turns back when I
turn back, beating me to the door.

It spoils my food and steals
my sleep, and mocks me, saying,
"Where is your God now?"

And so, like a widow, I lie down
after supper. If I lie down
or sit up it's all the same:

the days and nights bear me along.
To strangers I must seem
alive. Spring comes, summer;

cool, clear weather; heat, rain. . . .

Letter to Alice

Twilight. A few bats loop out of the barn,
dip and veer, feeding on flies and midges
in humid air. Before the storm
I top-dressed the perennials with manure,
ashes from the stove, and bone meal.
The rain soaking through the black
and white makes a mad, elemental tea.

I bought the bone meal up in New London,
where the streets are crowded for the summer
with stately Episcopalians – and I've noticed
that it hardly smells.

We made less than usual on the Church Fair supper,
held this year in the Blazing Star Grange,
because of rain. Down in the valley
we're land-rich but cash-poor, shorter,
stouter, and lower-church.

By now the blackflies are biting more out of habit
than desire, and graduation night is over.
I've picked up all the beer cans
from the pond road to the bridge.

The fully open peonies seem overcome by rain
and carnality. I should stake them: white
doubles with a raspberry fleck
at the heart, blooming without restraint
in the moist summer night. I planted them
just last fall, and this is a good showing
for their first year. More flowers, more art.
                                        Write!

After an Illness, Walking the Dog

Wet things smell stronger,
and I suppose his main regret is that
he can sniff just one at a time.
In a frenzy of delight
he runs way up the sandy road –
scored by freshets after five days
of rain. Every pebble gleams, every leaf.

When I whistle he halts abruptly
and steps in a circle,
swings his extravagant tail.
Then he rolls and rubs his muzzle
in a particular place, while the drizzle
falls without cease, and Queen Anne's lace
and goldenrod bend low.

The top of the logging road stands open
and bright. Another day, before
hunting starts, we'll see how far it goes,
leaving word first at home.
The footing is ambiguous.

Soaked and muddy, the dog drops,
panting, and looks up with what amounts
to a grin. It's so good to be uphill with him,
nicely winded, and looking down on the pond.

A sound commences in my left ear
like the sound of the sea in a shell;

a downward vertiginous drag comes with it.
Time to head home. I wait
until we're nearly out to the main road
to put him back on the leash, and he
–the designated optimist–
imagines to the end that he is free.

Wash Day

How it rained while you slept! Wakeful,
I wandered around feeling the sills,
followed closely by the dog and cat.
We conferred, and left a few windows
open a crack.
                    Now the morning is clear
and bright, the wooden clothespins
swollen after the wet night.

The monkshood has slipped its stakes
and the blue cloaks drag in the mud.
Even the daisies – goodhearted
simpletons – seem cast down.

We have reached and passed the zenith.
The irises, poppies, and peonies, and the old
shrub roses with their romantic names
and profound attars have gone by
like young men and women of promise
who end up living indifferent lives.

How is it that every object in this basket
got to be inside out? There must be
a trickster in the hamper, a backward,
unclean spirit.
                    The clothes – the thicker
things – may not get dry by dusk.
The days are getting shorter. . . .
You'll laugh, but I feel it –
some power has gone from the sun.

Geranium

How many years did I lug it, pale and leggy,
onto the porch for the summer? There its stems
turned thick, its leaves curly and dark,
and it bloomed almost immediately.

Before first frost I'd bring it back inside
where it yellowed like the soles of the feet
of someone very old. Its flowers fell apart.

One spring I cut back all but one shoot,
and that I tied against a bamboo stake
to make a long straight stem.
Then I pinched out the new growth repeatedly
until I had a full, round ball on a stick,
like topiary at Versailles. It pleased me well;
its flowers were salmon pink.

I fed it fish emulsion, bone meal, wood
ashes; mulched it with cocoa pod hulls,
gave it a Tuscan terra cotta pot.
It was my nightingale, my goose, my golden
child. We drank from the same cup.

After the night's downpour I find the top
snapped off, lying on the ground like a rack
of antlers. Not even wilted yet—I've come
upon the fresh disaster. . . . Like Beethoven's
head its head had grown too large.

Cultural Exchange

A postcard arrives from a friend
visiting the Great Wall of China.
"Life couldn't be better," says M.

I was there once, in March. Unkind wind
bore down from the north. Mongolia . . .
How steep it is! In places even presidents
are forced to drop down on all fours.

On the way back to Beijing
our embassy car rushed wildly
through a succession of hamlets, forcing
bicycles off the road, dooryard
fowl to flap and fluster, and from
grandmother, bundled in her blue jacket
to take the pale sun, such a look!

Tired? Tired was not the word.
Getting sleepy in the warm car
I considered the Wall, the scale
of enterprise. A lock of hair had fallen
across my eyes. At last my brain
convinced my hand to move it.

That night I was honored by a banquet
in a room so cold I could see my breath.

Homesick

My clothes and hair smell stale,
and more than once I have slept in my coat
on trains that crashed past isolated stations
where magnolias bloom all night
beside dusty platform benches.

Twice I bought dried fish rolled
in cellophane, thinking it was pastry.

Leaving the pebbled Buddhist garden
such a dreadful languor overtook me;
I could hardly step over the threshold.
The monks were eating bean curd
fixed eleven different ways
and drinking bowls of frothy bitter green tea.

Oh my bed, and the dear dust under it!
Bath towels that don't smell like miso soup;
my own little dog, one ear up
and one ear down, and a speaker of English;
the teller at the village bank
who never asks to see my passport . . .

"Yes," I'll say, "we had a wonderful time.
We slept on pillows filled with cotton seed,
ate cuttle fish, dried squid, and black bean
paste, and drank pink laurel wine."

Summer: 6:00 a.m.

From the shadowy upstairs bedroom
of my mother-in-law's house in Hamden
I hear the neighbors' children waking.

"Ahhhhhhhh," says the infant, not
unhappily. "Yes, yes, yes, yes, yes!"
replies the toddler to his mother,
who must have forbidden something.
It is hot already at this hour
and the houses are wholly open.
If she is cross with the child
anyone with ears will hear.

The slap of sprinkler water
hitting the sidewalk and street,
and the husband's deliberate footfalls
receding down the drive . . .

His Japanese sedan matches the house.
Beige, brown . . . Yesterday he washed it,
his arm thrust deep into something
that looked like a sheepskin oven mitt.

His wife had put the babies
in the shallow plastic wading
pool, and she took snapshots, trying
repeatedly to get both boys to look.
The older one's wail rose
and matched the pitch of the cicada
in a nearby tree. Why

is the sound of a spoon on a plate
next door a thing so desolate?
I think of the woman pouring a glass of juice
for the three-year-old, and watching him
spill it, knowing he *must* spill it,
seeing the ineluctable downward course
of the orange-pink liquid, the puddle
swell on the kitchen
floor beside the child's shoe.

Walking Notes: Hamden, Connecticut

Wearing only her nightdress
with a white sweater thrown over her shoulders,
a woman stands at the curb, watching
with a look of love and patience
as her aged poodle snuffles at a candy wrapper.
I see her as her husband of forty years
sees her: hair tied back by a broad, pink
ribbon, eyes swollen with sleep.

My daily walk takes me past a house
where roses scramble lustily
up the trellises, a Dorothy Perkins
and a climbing Peace. Stuffed animals
look out from the sunroom window sills.

The house where two dentists, Dr. Charles Molloy
and Dr. Everett Condon, drill and pack . . .
The boys in the neighborhood call Dr. Condon
Dr. Condom. They know all about such things
though their parents have told them little
about sex, leaving that to luck, or the lack
of it, or lurid films on hygiene in gym class.

The girl next door, a real beauty, her long black
curls drawn up with combs like someone in Turgenev,
waters the lawn, not thoroughly. Her father
is about to be indicted for racketeering.
For a long time they didn't mow. The wind
carried weed seeds into the neighbors' yards.
Everyone was irate. . . . Then suddenly
he mowed, and now she waters listlessly.

Last Days

Over the orchard a truly black cloud appeared.
Then horizontal rain began, and apples fell
before their time. Leaves blew
in phalanxes along the ground. Doors
opened and closed of their own accord. The lights
went out, but then thought better of it.

So I sat with her in a room made small
by the paraphernalia of the mortally ill.
Among ranks of brown bottles from the pharmacy
a hymnbook lay open on the chest of drawers:
"Safely Through Another Week." Indifferent,
a housefly lit on her blue-white brow.

Looking at Stars

The God of curved space, the dry
God, is not going to help us, but the son
whose blood spattered
the hem of his mother's robe.

At the Dime Store

Since I saw him last his teeth have gone.
The gaps draw my eyes, and like Saint
Paul I give way: that very thing I would
not do, I do. He notices, abashed.

Most of one summer he was around, coming
by seven each morning with his rascally look
to build a new wing and replace the old
north sill. Sometimes he'd disappear for a day
or a week. There was trouble at home
and on his lunch hour he'd call—just over
the town line and so long distance—
thinking we couldn't hear or wouldn't
care. This was years ago.

When I encounter him again in the aisles
we both grin shyly. His boy, tall suddenly,
and bulky, not built like his father at all,
joins him at the check-out.
They've got an aquarium in their cart.

At last the job was finished. All but
taking up the piles of extra shingles,
sawhorses, and lumber from the back
yard. Weeks passed. I called. Yes,
his wife assured me, he'd be coming by.

And finally one day he did
while I was up in town having a filling
replaced. When I got home, shaky
and feeling mussed, I saw that everything
of substance was gone, leaving only
white rectangular spaces on the lawn.

Let Evening Come

Let the light of late afternoon
shine through chinks in the barn, moving
up the bales as the sun moves down.

Let the cricket take up chafing
as a woman takes up her needles
and her yarn. Let evening come.

Let dew collect on the hoe abandoned
in long grass. Let the stars appear
and the moon disclose her silver horn.

Let the fox go back to its sandy den.
Let the wind die down. Let the shed
go black inside. Let evening come.

To the bottle in the ditch, to the scoop
in the oats, to air in the lung
let evening come.

Let it come, as it will, and don't
be afraid. God does not leave us
comfortless, so let evening come.

With the Dog at Sunrise

Although we always come this way
I never noticed before that the poplars
growing along the ravine
shine pink in the light of winter dawn.

What am I going to say
in my letter to Sarah – a widow
at thirty-one, alone in the violence
of her grief, sleepless,
and utterly cast down?

I look at the lithe, pink trees more carefully,
remembering Stephen, the photographer.
With the hunger of two I take them in.
Perhaps I can tell her that.

The dog furrows his brow while pissing long
and thoughtfully against an ancient hemlock.
The snow turns the saffron of a monk's robe
and acrid steam ascends.

Searching for God is the first thing and the last,
but in between such trouble, and such pain.

Far up in the woods where no one goes
deer take their ease under the great
pines, nose to steaming nose. . . .

This book was designed by Tree Swenson.
The Bembo type was set by The Typeworks.
Manufactured by Thomson-Shore.